POPE FRANCIS TALKS TO COUPLES

WISDOM ON MARRIAGE AND FAMILY

Excerpt from *Amoris Laetitia,* The Joy of Love

POPE FRANCIS

Paulist Press
New York / Mahwah, NJ

Library of Congress Control Number: 2016943965

ISBN 978-0-8091-5325-1 (paperback)

Published by Paulist Press
997 Macarthur Boulevard
Mahwah, New Jersey 07430

www.paulistpress.com

Printed and bound in the United States of America

CONTENTS

PUBLISHER'S NOTE

Pope Francis keeps a special place in his heart for married couples. These two chapters, drawn from his much larger letter *The Joy of Love: On Love in the Family*, are dedicated to couples. Because he expressly suggests that couples read chapters four and five from *The Joy of Love*, we have printed them separately. In many ways, they are his conversation with couples: those thinking about marriage, those newly married, those living their marriage. Reading these chapters, you can imagine him sitting in your living room, or at your kitchen table, sipping a cup of coffee, listening to you talk about your relationship, sharing his wisdom, offering you encouragement and hope.

This is not the sort of book you read all the way through. The pope encourages you to read paragraphs together, and when something strikes you as important, to stop and talk to each other about what it means to you and, above all, to listen to what it means to your partner. Pope Francis encourages couples to dialogue and hopes these pages become an opportunity for you to dialogue with each other and with God.

Pastoral ministers who work in Pre-Cana, Marriage Encounter, and marriage enrichment programs will find in these words of Pope Francis an inspiring pastoral resource for the couples they serve.

"No family drops down from heaven perfectly formed; families need to constantly grow and mature in the ability to love," Pope Francis writes; we hope that this little book helps couples grow and mature in love.

Fr. Mark-David Janus, CSP
President and Publisher, Paulist Press

LOVE IN MARRIAGE

89.   All that has been said so far would be insufficient to express the Gospel of marriage and the family, were we not also to *speak of love*. For we cannot encourage a path of fidelity and mutual self-giving without encouraging the growth, strengthening and deepening of conjugal and family love. Indeed, the grace of the sacrament of marriage is intended before all else "to perfect the couple's love".[104] Here too we can say that, "even if I have faith so as to remove mountains, but have not love, I am nothing. If I give all I have, and if I deliver my body to be burned, but have not love, I gain nothing" (*1 Cor* 13:2-3). The word "love", however, is commonly used and often misused.[105]

Our daily love

90.   In a lyrical passage of Saint Paul, we see some of the features of true love:

---

[104] Catechism of the Catholic Church, 1641.
[105] Cf. BENEDICT XVI, Encyclical Letter *Deus Caritas Est* (25 December 2005), 2: AAS 98 (2006), 218.

"Love is patient,
love is kind;
love is not jealous or boastful;
it is not arrogant or rude.
Love does not insist on its own way,
it is not irritable or resentful;
it does not rejoice at wrong,
but rejoices in the right.
Love bears all things,
believes all things,
hopes all things,
endures all things" (*1 Cor* 13:4-7).

Love is experienced and nurtured in the daily life of couples and their children. It is helpful to think more deeply about the meaning of this Pauline text and its relevance for the concrete situation of every family.

Love is patient

91. The first word used is *makrothyméi.* This does not simply have to do with "enduring all things", because we find that idea expressed at the end of the seventh verse. Its meaning is clarified by the Greek translation of the Old Testament, where we read that God is "slow to anger" (*Ex* 34:6; *Num* 14:18). It refers, then, to the quality of one who does not act on impulse and avoids giving offense. We find this quality in the God of the Covenant, who calls us to imitate him also within the life of the family. Saint Paul's texts using this word need to be read in the light of the Book of Wisdom (cf. 11:23; 12:2, 15-18), which

extols God's restraint, as leaving open the possibility of repentance, yet insists on his power, as revealed in his acts of mercy. God's "patience", shown in his mercy towards sinners, is a sign of his real power.

92. Being patient does not mean letting ourselves be constantly mistreated, tolerating physical aggression or allowing other people to use us. We encounter problems whenever we think that relationships or people ought to be perfect, or when we put ourselves at the centre and expect things to turn out our way. Then everything makes us impatient, everything makes us react aggressively. Unless we cultivate patience, we will always find excuses for responding angrily. We will end up incapable of living together, antisocial, unable to control our impulses, and our families will become battlegrounds. That is why the word of God tells us: "Let all bitterness and wrath and anger and clamour and slander be put away from you, with all malice" (*Eph* 4:31). Patience takes root when I recognize that other people also have a right to live in this world, just as they are. It does not matter if they hold me back, if they unsettle my plans, or annoy me by the way they act or think, or if they are not everything I want them to be. Love always has an aspect of deep compassion that leads to accepting the other person as part of this world, even when he or she acts differently than I would like.

Love is at the service of others

93. The next word that Paul uses is *chrestéuetai*. The word is used only here in the entire Bible. It is

3

derived from *chrestós*: a good person, one who shows his goodness by his deeds. Here, in strict parallelism with the preceding verb, it serves as a complement. Paul wants to make it clear that "patience" is not a completely passive attitude, but one accompanied by activity, by a dynamic and creative interaction with others. The word indicates that love benefits and helps others. For this reason it is translated as "kind"; love is ever ready to be of assistance.

94.   Throughout the text, it is clear that Paul wants to stress that love is more than a mere feeling. Rather, it should be understood along the lines of the Hebrew verb "to love"; it is "to do good". As Saint Ignatius of Loyola said, "Love is shown more by deeds than by words".[106] It thus shows its fruitfulness and allows us to experience the happiness of giving, the nobility and grandeur of spending ourselves unstintingly, without asking to be repaid, purely for the pleasure of giving and serving.

Love is not jealous

95.   Saint Paul goes on to reject as contrary to love an attitude expressed by the verb *zelói* – to be jealous or envious. This means that love has no room for discomfiture at another person's good fortune (cf. *Acts* 7:9; 17:5). Envy is a form of sadness provoked by another's prosperity; it shows that we are not concerned for the happiness of others but only with our own well-being. Whereas love makes us rise above ourselves, envy closes

---

[106] *Spiritual Exercises,* Contemplation to Attain Love (230).

us in on ourselves. True love values the other person's achievements. It does not see him or her as a threat. It frees us from the sour taste of envy. It recognizes that everyone has different gifts and a unique path in life. So it strives to discover its own road to happiness, while allowing others to find theirs.

96. In a word, love means fulfilling the last two commandments of God's Law: "You shall not covet your neighbour's house; you shall not covet your neighbour's wife, or his manservant, or his maidservant, or his ox, or his donkey, or anything that is your neighbour's" (*Ex* 20:17). Love inspires a sincere esteem for every human being and the recognition of his or her own right to happiness. I love this person, and I see him or her with the eyes of God, who gives us everything "for our enjoyment" (*1 Tim* 6:17). As a result, I feel a deep sense of happiness and peace. This same deeply rooted love also leads me to reject the injustice whereby some possess too much and others too little. It moves me to find ways of helping society's outcasts to find a modicum of joy. That is not envy, but the desire for equality.

Love is not boastful

97. The following word, *perpereúetai*, denotes vainglory, the need to be haughty, pedantic and somewhat pushy. Those who love not only refrain from speaking too much about themselves, but are focused on others; they do not need to be the centre of attention. The word that comes next – *physioútai* – is similar, indicating that love is not arrogant. Literally, it means

5

that we do not become "puffed up" before others. It also points to something more subtle: an obsession with showing off and a loss of a sense of reality. Such people think that, because they are more "spiritual" or "wise", they are more important than they really are. Paul uses this verb on other occasions, as when he says that "knowledge puffs up", whereas "love builds up" (*1 Cor* 8:1). Some think that they are important because they are more knowledgeable than others; they want to lord it over them. Yet what really makes us important is a love that understands, shows concern, and embraces the weak. Elsewhere the word is used to criticize those who are "inflated" with their own importance (cf. *1 Cor* 4:18) but in fact are filled more with empty words than the real "power" of the Spirit (cf. *1 Cor* 4:19).

98.   It is important for Christians to show their love by the way they treat family members who are less knowledgeable about the faith, weak or less sure in their convictions. At times the opposite occurs: the supposedly mature believers within the family become unbearably arrogant. Love, on the other hand, is marked by humility; if we are to understand, forgive and serve others from the heart, our pride has to be healed and our humility must increase. Jesus told his disciples that in a world where power prevails, each tries to dominate the other, but "it shall not be so among you" (*Mt* 20:26). The inner logic of Christian love is not about importance and power; rather, "whoever would be first among you must be your slave" (*Mt* 20:27). In family life, the logic of domination and

competition about who is the most intelligent or powerful destroys love. Saint Peter's admonition also applies to the family: "Clothe yourselves, all of you, with humility towards one another, for 'God opposes the proud, but gives grace to the humble'" (*1 Pet* 5:5).

Love is not rude

99.   To love is also to be gentle and thoughtful, and this is conveyed by the next word, *aschemonéi*. It indicates that love is not rude or impolite; it is not harsh. Its actions, words and gestures are pleasing and not abrasive or rigid.   Love abhors making others suffer. Courtesy "is a school of sensitivity and disinterestedness" which requires a person "to develop his or her mind and feelings, learning how to listen, to speak and, at certain times, to keep quiet".[107]   It is not something that a Christian may accept or reject.   As an essential requirement of love, "every human being is bound to live agreeably with those around him".[108] Every day, "entering into the life of another, even when that person already has a part to play in our life, demands the sensitivity and restraint which can renew trust and respect.   Indeed, the deeper love is, the more it calls for respect for the other's freedom and the ability to wait until the other opens the door to his or her heart".[109]

---

[107]   Octavio Paz, *La llama doble*, Barcelona, 1993, 35.
[108]   Thomas Aquinas, *Summa Theologiae* II-II, q. 114, art. 2, ad 1.
[109]   Catechesis (13 May 2005): *L'Osservatore Romano*, 14 May 2015, p. 8.

100.   To be open to a genuine encounter with others, "a kind look" is essential. This is incompatible with a negative attitude that readily points out other people's shortcomings while overlooking one's own. A kind look helps us to see beyond our own limitations, to be patient and to cooperate with others, despite our differences. Loving kindness builds bonds, cultivates relationships, creates new networks of integration and knits a firm social fabric. In this way, it grows ever stronger, for without a sense of belonging we cannot sustain a commitment to others; we end up seeking our convenience alone and life in common becomes impossible. Antisocial persons think that others exist only for the satisfaction of their own needs. Consequently, there is no room for the gentleness of love and its expression. Those who love are capable of speaking words of comfort, strength, consolation, and encouragement. These were the words that Jesus himself spoke: "Take heart, my son!" (*Mt* 9:2); "Great is your faith!" (*Mt* 15:28); "Arise!" (*Mk* 5:41); "Go in peace" (*Lk* 7:50); "Be not afraid" (*Mt* 14:27). These are not words that demean, sadden, anger or show scorn. In our families, we must learn to imitate Jesus' own gentleness in our way of speaking to one another.

Love is generous

101.   We have repeatedly said that to love another we must first love ourselves. Paul's hymn to love, however, states that love "does not seek its own interest", nor "seek what is its own". This same idea is expressed in another text: "Let each of you look not

only to his own interests, but also to the interests of others" (*Phil* 2:4). The Bible makes it clear that generously serving others is far more noble than loving ourselves. Loving ourselves is only important as a psychological prerequisite for being able to love others: "If a man is mean to himself, to whom will he be generous? No one is meaner than the man who is grudging to himself" (*Sir* 14:5-6).

102. Saint Thomas Aquinas explains that "it is more proper to charity to desire to love than to desire to be loved";[110] indeed, "mothers, who are those who love the most, seek to love more than to be loved".[111] Consequently, love can transcend and overflow the demands of justice, "expecting nothing in return" (*Lk* 6:35), and the greatest of loves can lead to "laying down one's life" for another (cf. *Jn* 15:13). Can such generosity, which enables us to give freely and fully, really be possible? Yes, because it is demanded by the Gospel: "You received without pay, give without pay" (*Mt* 10:8).

Love is not irritable or resentful

103. If the first word of Paul's hymn spoke of the need for a patience that does not immediately react harshly to the weaknesses and faults of others, the word he uses next – *paroxýnetai* – has to do more

---

[110] THOMAS AQUINAS, *Summa Theologiae*, II-II, q. 27, art. 1, ad 2.
[111] *Ibid.*, q. 27, art. 1.

with an interior indignation provoked by something from without. It refers to a violent reaction within, a hidden irritation that sets us on edge where others are concerned, as if they were troublesome or threatening and thus to be avoided. To nurture such interior hostility helps no one. It only causes hurt and alienation. Indignation is only healthy when it makes us react to a grave injustice; when it permeates our attitude towards others it is harmful.

104.   The Gospel tells us to look to the log in our own eye (cf. *Mt* 7:5). Christians cannot ignore the persistent admonition of God's word not to nurture anger: "Do not be overcome by evil" (*Rm* 12:21). "Let us not grow weary in doing good" (*Gal* 6:9). It is one thing to sense a sudden surge of hostility and another to give into it, letting it take root in our hearts: "Be angry but do not sin; do not let the sun go down on your anger" (*Eph* 4:26). My advice is never to let the day end without making peace in the family. "And how am I going to make peace? By getting down on my knees? No! Just by a small gesture, a little something, and harmony within your family will be restored. Just a little caress, no words are necessary. But do not let the day end without making peace in your family".[112] Our first reaction when we are annoyed should be one of heartfelt blessing, asking God to bless, free and heal that person. "On the contrary bless, for to this you have been called, that

---

[112] Catechesis (13 May 2015): *L'Osservatore Romano*, 14 May 2015, p. 8.

you may obtain a blessing" (*1 Pet* 3:9). If we must fight evil, so be it; but we must always say "no" to violence in the home.

Love forgives

105. Once we allow ill will to take root in our hearts, it leads to deep resentment. The phrase *ou logízetai to kakón* means that love "takes no account of evil"; "it is not resentful". The opposite of resentment is forgiveness, which is rooted in a positive attitude that seeks to understand other people's weaknesses and to excuse them. As Jesus said, "Father, forgive them; for they know not what they do" (*Lk* 23:34). Yet we keep looking for more and more faults, imagining greater evils, presuming all kinds of bad intentions, and so resentment grows and deepens. Thus, every mistake or lapse on the part of a spouse can harm the bond of love and the stability of the family. Something is wrong when we see every problem as equally serious; in this way, we risk being unduly harsh with the failings of others. The just desire to see our rights respected turns into a thirst for vengeance rather than a reasoned defence of our dignity.

106. When we have been offended or let down, forgiveness is possible and desirable, but no one can say that it is easy. The truth is that "family communion can only be preserved and perfected through a great spirit of sacrifice. It requires, in fact, a ready and generous openness of each and all to understanding, to forbearance, to pardon, to reconciliation. There is no

family that does not know how selfishness, discord, tension and conflict violently attack and at times mortally wound its own communion: hence there arise the many and varied forms of division in family life".[113]

107. Today we recognize that being able to forgive others implies the liberating experience of understanding and forgiving ourselves. Often our mistakes, or criticism we have received from loved ones, can lead to a loss of self-esteem. We become distant from others, avoiding affection and fearful in our interpersonal relationships. Blaming others becomes falsely reassuring. We need to learn to pray over our past history, to accept ourselves, to learn how to live with our limitations, and even to forgive ourselves, in order to have this same attitude towards others.

108. All this assumes that we ourselves have had the experience of being forgiven by God, justified by his grace and not by our own merits. We have known a love that is prior to any of our own efforts, a love that constantly opens doors, promotes and encourages. If we accept that God's love is unconditional, that the Father's love cannot be bought or sold, then we will become capable of showing boundless love and forgiving others even if they have wronged us. Otherwise, our family life will no longer be a place of understanding, support and encouragement, but rather one of constant tension and mutual criticism.

[113] JOHN PAUL II, Apostolic Exhortation *Familiaris Consortio* (22 November 1981), 21: AAS 74 (1982), 106.

Love rejoices with others

109.   The expression *chaírei epì te adikía* has to do with a negativity lurking deep within a person's heart. It is the toxic attitude of those who rejoice at seeing an injustice done to others. The following phrase expresses its opposite: *sygchaírei te aletheía*: "it rejoices in the right". In other words, we rejoice at the good of others when we see their dignity and value their abilities and good works. This is impossible for those who must always be comparing and competing, even with their spouse, so that they secretly rejoice in their failures.

110.   When a loving person can do good for others, or sees that others are happy, they themselves live happily and in this way give glory to God, for "God loves a cheerful giver" (*2 Cor* 9:7). Our Lord especially appreciates those who find joy in the happiness of others. If we fail to learn how to rejoice in the well-being of others, and focus primarily on our own needs, we condemn ourselves to a joyless existence, for, as Jesus said, "it is more blessed to give than to receive" (*Acts* 20:35). The family must always be a place where, when something good happens to one of its members, they know that others will be there to celebrate it with them.

Love bears all things

111.   Paul's list ends with four phrases containing the words "all things". Love bears all things, believes all things, hopes all things, endures all things. Here

we see clearly the countercultural power of a love that is able to face whatever might threaten it.

112.   First, Paul says that love "bears all things" (*panta stégei*). This is about more than simply putting up with evil; it has to do with *the use of the tongue*. The verb can mean "holding one's peace" about what may be wrong with another person.   It implies limiting judgment, checking the impulse to issue a firm and ruthless condemnation: "Judge not and you will not be judged" (*Lk* 6:37).   Although it runs contrary to the way we normally use our tongues, God's word tells us: "Do not speak evil against one another, brothers and sisters" (*Jas* 4:11).   Being willing to speak ill of another person is a way of asserting ourselves, venting resentment and envy without concern for the harm we may do.   We often forget that slander can be quite sinful; it is a grave offense against God when it seriously harms another person's good name and causes damage that is hard to repair.   Hence God's word forthrightly states that the tongue "is a world of iniquity" that "stains the whole body" (*Jas* 3:6); it is a "restless evil, full of deadly poison" (3:8).   Whereas the tongue can be used to "curse those who are made in the likeness of God" (3:9), love cherishes the good name of others, even one's enemies. In seeking to uphold God's law we must never forget this specific requirement of love.

113.   Married couples joined by love speak well of each other; they try to show their spouse's good side, not their weakness and faults.   In any event, they keep silent rather than speak ill of them.   This is not merely

a way of acting in front of others; it springs from an interior attitude. Far from ingenuously claiming not to see the problems and weaknesses of others, it sees those weaknesses and faults in a wider context. It recognizes that these failings are a part of a bigger picture. We have to realize that all of us are a complex mixture of light and shadows. The other person is much more than the sum of the little things that annoy me. Love does not have to be perfect for us to value it. The other person loves me as best they can, with all their limits, but the fact that love is imperfect does not mean that it is untrue or unreal. It is real, albeit limited and earthly. If I expect too much, the other person will let me know, for he or she can neither play God nor serve all my needs. Love coexists with imperfection. It "bears all things" and can hold its peace before the limitations of the loved one.

Love believes all things

114.   *Panta pisteúei.* Love believes all things. Here "belief" is not to be taken in its strict theological meaning, but more in the sense of what we mean by "trust". This goes beyond simply presuming that the other is not lying or cheating. Such basic trust recognizes God's light shining beyond the darkness, like an ember glowing beneath the ash.

115.   This trust enables a relationship to be free. It means we do not have to control the other person, to follow their every step lest they escape our grip. Love trusts, it sets free, it does not try to control, possess

and dominate everything. This freedom, which fosters independence, an openness to the world around us and to new experiences, can only enrich and expand relationships. The spouses then share with one another the joy of all they have received and learned outside the family circle. At the same time, this freedom makes for sincerity and transparency, for those who know that they are trusted and appreciated can be open and hide nothing. Those who know that their spouse is always suspicious, judgmental and lacking unconditional love, will tend to keep secrets, conceal their failings and weaknesses, and pretend to be someone other than who they are. On the other hand, a family marked by loving trust, come what may, helps its members to be themselves and spontaneously to reject deceit, falsehood, and lies.

Love hopes all things

116.   *Panta elpízei.* Love does not despair of the future. Following upon what has just been said, this phrase speaks of the hope of one who knows that others can change, mature and radiate unexpected beauty and untold potential. This does not mean that everything will change in this life. It does involve realizing that, though things may not always turn out as we wish, God may well make crooked lines straight and draw some good from the evil we endure in this world.

117.   Here hope comes most fully into its own, for it embraces the certainty of life after death. Each person, with all his or her failings, is called to the fullness of life

in heaven. There, fully transformed by Christ's resurrection, every weakness, darkness and infirmity will pass away. There the person's true being will shine forth in all its goodness and beauty. This realization helps us, amid the aggravations of this present life, to see each person from a supernatural perspective, in the light of hope, and await the fullness that he or she will receive in the heavenly kingdom, even if it is not yet visible.

Love endures all things

118. *Panta hypoménei.* This means that love bears every trial with a positive attitude. It stands firm in hostile surroundings. This "endurance" involves not only the ability to tolerate certain aggravations, but something greater: a constant readiness to confront any challenge. It is a love that *never gives up*, even in the darkest hour. It shows a certain dogged heroism, a power to resist every negative current, an irrepressible commitment to goodness. Here I think of the words of Martin Luther King, who met every kind of trial and tribulation with fraternal love: "The person who hates you most has some good in him; even the nation that hates you most has some good in it; even the race that hates you most has some good in it. And when you come to the point that you look in the face of every man and see deep down within him what religion calls 'the image of God', you begin to love him in spite of [everything]. No matter what he does, you see God's image there. There is an element of goodness that he can never sluff off... Another way that you love your enemy is this: when the

opportunity presents itself for you to defeat your enemy, that is the time which you must not do it… When you rise to the level of love, of its great beauty and power, you seek only to defeat evil systems. Individuals who happen to be caught up in that system, you love, but you seek to defeat the system… Hate for hate only intensifies the existence of hate and evil in the universe. If I hit you and you hit me and I hit you back and you hit me back and so on, you see, that goes on ad infinitum. It just never ends. Somewhere somebody must have a little sense, and that's the strong person. The strong person is the person who can cut off the chain of hate, the chain of evil… Somebody must have religion enough and morality enough to cut it off and inject within the very structure of the universe that strong and powerful element of love".[114]

119.   In family life, we need to cultivate that strength of love which can help us fight every evil threatening it. Love does not yield to resentment, scorn for others or the desire to hurt or to gain some advantage. The Christian ideal, especially in families, is a love that never gives up. I am sometimes amazed to see men or women who have had to separate from their spouse for their own protection, yet, because of their enduring conjugal love, still try to help them, even by enlisting others, in their moments of illness, suffering or trial. Here too we see a love that never gives up.

[114] MARTIN LUTHER KING JR., *Sermon delivered at Dexter Avenue Baptist Church*, Montgomery, Alabama, 17 November 1957.

120. Our reflection on Saint Paul's hymn to love has prepared us to discuss conjugal love. This is the love between husband and wife,[115] a love sanctified, enriched and illuminated by the grace of the sacrament of marriage. It is an "affective union",[116] spiritual and sacrificial, which combines the warmth of friendship and erotic passion, and endures long after emotions and passion subside. Pope Pius XI taught that this love permeates the duties of married life and enjoys pride of place.[117] Infused by the Holy Spirit, this powerful love is a reflection of the unbroken covenant between Christ and humanity that culminated in his self-sacrifice on the cross. "The Spirit which the Lord pours forth gives a new heart and renders man and woman capable of loving one another as Christ loved us. Conjugal love reaches that fullness to which it is interiorly ordained: conjugal charity."[118]

121. Marriage is a precious sign, for "when a man and a woman celebrate the sacrament of marriage, God is, as it were, 'mirrored' in them; he impresses in them his own features and the indelible character of his love. Marriage is the icon of God's love for us.

[115] Thomas Aquinas calls love a *vis unitiva* (*Summa Theologiae* I, q. 20, art. 1, ad 3), echoing a phrase of Pseudo-Dionysius the Areopagite (*De Divinis Nominibus*, IV, 12: PG 3, 709).

[116] THOMAS AQUINAS, *Summa Theologiae* II-II, q. 27, art. 2.

[117] Encyclical Letter *Casti Connubii* (31 December 1930): AAS 22 (1930), 547-548.

[118] JOHN PAUL II, Apostolic Exhortation *Familiaris Consortio* (22 November 1981) 13: AAS 74 (1982), 94.

Indeed, God is also communion: the three Persons of the Father, the Son and the Holy Spirit live eternally in perfect unity. And this is precisely the mystery of marriage: God makes of the two spouses one single existence".[119] This has concrete daily consequences, because the spouses, "in virtue of the sacrament, are invested with a true and proper mission, so that, starting with the simple ordinary things of life they can make visible the love with which Christ loves his Church and continues to give his life for her".[120]

122. We should not however confuse different levels: there is no need to lay upon two limited persons the tremendous burden of having to reproduce perfectly the union existing between Christ and his Church, for marriage as a sign entails "a dynamic process..., one which advances gradually with the progressive integration of the gifts of God".[121]

Lifelong sharing

123. After the love that unites us to God, conjugal love is the "greatest form of friendship".[122] It is a union possessing all the traits of a good friendship: concern for the good of the other, reciprocity, intimacy, warmth,

---

[119] Catechesis (2 April 2014): *L'Osservatore Romano*, 3 April 2014, p. 8.

[120] *Ibid.*

[121] JOHN PAUL II, Apostolic Exhortation *Familiaris Consortio* (22 November 1981), 9: AAS 75 (1982), 90.

[122] THOMAS AQUINAS, *Summa Contra Gentiles* III, 123; cf. ARISTOTLE, *Nicomachean Ethics*, 8, 12 (ed. Bywater, Oxford, 1984, 174).

stability and the resemblance born of a shared life. Marriage joins to all this an indissoluble exclusivity expressed in the stable commitment to share and shape together the whole of life. Let us be honest and acknowledge the signs that this is the case. Lovers do not see their relationship as merely temporary. Those who marry do not expect their excitement to fade. Those who witness the celebration of a loving union, however fragile, trust that it will pass the test of time. Children not only want their parents to love one another, but also to be faithful and remain together. These and similar signs show that it is in the very nature of conjugal love to be definitive. The lasting union expressed by the marriage vows is more than a formality or a traditional formula; it is rooted in the natural inclinations of the human person. For believers, it is also a covenant before God that calls for fidelity: "The Lord was witness to the covenant between you and the wife of your youth, to whom you have been faithless, though she is your companion and your wife by covenant... Let none be faithless to the wife of his youth. For I hate divorce, says the Lord" (*Mal* 2:14-16).

124. A love that is weak or infirm, incapable of accepting marriage as a challenge to be taken up and fought for, reborn, renewed and reinvented until death, cannot sustain a great commitment. It will succumb to the culture of the ephemeral that prevents a constant process of growth. Yet "promising love for ever is possible when we perceive a plan bigger than our own ideas and undertakings, a plan which sustains us and enables us to surrender our future entirely to the one

we love".[123]   If this love is to overcome all trials and remain faithful in the face of everything, it needs the gift of grace to strengthen and elevate it. In the words of Saint Robert Bellarmine, "the fact that one man unites with one woman in an indissoluble bond, and that they remain inseparable despite every kind of difficulty, even when there is no longer hope for children, can only be the sign of a great mystery".[124]

125.   Marriage is likewise a friendship marked by passion, but a passion always directed to an ever more stable and intense union. This is because "marriage was not instituted solely for the procreation of children" but also that mutual love "might be properly expressed, that it should grow and mature".[125] This unique friendship between a man and a woman acquires an all-encompassing character only within the conjugal union. Precisely as all-encompassing, this union is also exclusive, faithful and open to new life. It shares everything in constant mutual respect. The Second Vatican Council echoed this by stating that "such a love, bringing together the human and the divine, leads the partners to a free and mutual self-giving, experienced in tenderness and action, and permeating their entire lives".[126]

---

[123]   Encyclical Letter *Lumen Fidei* (29 June 2013), 52: AAS 105 (2013), 590.
[124]   *De sacramento matrimonii*, I, 2; in ID., *Disputationes*, III, 5, 3 (ed. Giuliano, Naples, 1858), 778.
[125]   SECOND VATICAN ECUMENICAL COUNCIL, Pastoral Constitution on the Church in the Modern World *Gaudium et Spes*, 50.
[126]   *Ibid.*, 49.

Joy and beauty

126.   In marriage, the joy of love needs to be cultivated. When the search for pleasure becomes obsessive,
it holds us in thrall and keeps us from experiencing
other satisfactions. Joy, on the other hand, increases
our pleasure and helps us find fulfilment in any number of things, even at those times of life when physical
pleasure has ebbed. Saint Thomas Aquinas said that
the word "joy" refers to an expansion of the heart.[127]
Marital joy can be experienced even amid sorrow; it
involves accepting that marriage is an inevitable
mixture of enjoyment and struggles, tensions and
repose, pain and relief, satisfactions and longings,
annoyances and pleasures, but always on the path of
friendship, which inspires married couples to care for
one another: "they help and serve each other".[128]

127.   The love of friendship is called "charity" when
it perceives and esteems the "great worth" of another
person.[129] Beauty – that "great worth" which is other
than physical or psychological appeal – enables us to
appreciate the sacredness of a person, without feeling
the need to possess it. In a consumerist society, the
sense of beauty is impoverished and so joy fades.
Everything is there to be purchased, possessed or con-
sumed, including people. Tenderness, on the other
hand, is a sign of a love free of selfish possessiveness.

---

[127] Cf. *Summa Theologiae* I-II, q. 31, art. 3., ad 3.
[128] SECOND VATICAN ECUMENICAL COUNCIL, Pastoral Constitution on the Church in the Modern World *Gaudium et Spes*, 48.
[129] Cf. THOMAS AQUINAS, *Summa Theologiae* I-II, q. 26, art. 3.

It makes us approach a person with immense respect and a certain dread of causing them harm or taking away their freedom. Loving another person involves the joy of contemplating and appreciating their innate beauty and sacredness, which is greater than my needs. This enables me to seek their good even when they cannot belong to me, or when they are no longer physically appealing but intrusive and annoying. For "the love by which one person is pleasing to another depends on his or her giving something freely".[130]

128.   The aesthetic experience of love is expressed in that "gaze" which contemplates other persons as ends in themselves, even if they are infirm, elderly or physically unattractive.   A look of appreciation has enormous importance, and to begrudge it is usually hurtful.   How many things do spouses and children sometimes do in order to be noticed!   Much hurt and many problems result when we stop looking at one another.   This lies behind the complaints and grievances we often hear in families: "My husband does not look at me; he acts as if I were invisible".   "Please look at me when I am talking to you!".   "My wife no longer looks at me, she only has eyes for our children".   "In my own home nobody cares about me; they do not even see me; it is as if I did not exist".   Love opens our eyes and enables us to see, beyond all else, the great worth of a human being.

129.   The joy of this contemplative love needs to be cultivated.   Since we were made for love, we know

<hr />

[130]   *Ibid.*, q. 110, art. 1.

that there is no greater joy than that of sharing good things: "Give, take, and treat yourself well" (*Sir* 14:16). The most intense joys in life arise when we are able to elicit joy in others, as a foretaste of heaven. We can think of the lovely scene in the film *Babette's Feast*, when the generous cook receives a grateful hug and praise: "*Ah, how you will delight the angels!*" It is a joy and a great consolation to bring delight to others, to see them enjoying themselves. This joy, the fruit of fraternal love, is not that of the vain and self-centred, but of lovers who delight in the good of those whom they love, who give freely to them and thus bear good fruit.

130. On the other hand, joy also grows through pain and sorrow. In the words of Saint Augustine, "the greater the danger in battle the greater is the joy of victory".[131] After suffering and struggling together, spouses are able to experience that it was worth it, because they achieved some good, learned something as a couple, or came to appreciate what they have. Few human joys are as deep and thrilling as those experienced by two people who love one another and have achieved something as the result of a great, shared effort.

Marrying for love

131. I would like to say to young people that none of this is jeopardized when their love finds expression

---

[131] Augustine, *Confessions*, VIII, III, 7: PL 32, 752.

in marriage. Their union encounters in this institution the means to ensure that their love truly will endure and grow. Naturally, love is much more than an outward consent or a contract, yet it is nonetheless true that choosing to give marriage a visible form in society by undertaking certain commitments shows how important it is. It manifests the seriousness of each person's identification with the other and their firm decision to leave adolescent individualism behind and to belong to one another. Marriage is a means of expressing that we have truly left the security of the home in which we grew up in order to build other strong ties and to take on a new responsibility for another person. This is much more meaningful than a mere spontaneous association for mutual gratification, which would turn marriage into a purely private affair. As a social institution, marriage protects and shapes a shared commitment to deeper growth in love and commitment to one another, for the good of society as a whole. That is why marriage is more than a fleeting fashion; it is of enduring importance. Its essence derives from our human nature and social character. It involves a series of obligations born of love itself, a love so serious and generous that it is ready to face any risk.

132. To opt for marriage in this way expresses a genuine and firm decision to join paths, come what may. Given its seriousness, this public commitment of love cannot be the fruit of a hasty decision, but neither can it be postponed indefinitely. Committing oneself exclusively and definitively to another person always involves a risk and a bold gamble. Unwilling-

ness to make such a commitment is selfish, calculating and petty. It fails to recognize the rights of another person and to present him or her to society as someone worthy of unconditional love. If two persons are truly in love, they naturally show this to others. When love is expressed before others in the marriage contract, with all its public commitments, it clearly indicates and protects the "yes" which those persons speak freely and unreservedly to each other. This "yes" tells them that they can always trust one another, and that they will never be abandoned when difficulties arise or new attractions or selfish interests present themselves.

A love that reveals itself and increases

133.   The love of friendship unifies all aspects of marital life and helps family members to grow constantly.   This love must be freely and generously expressed in words and acts.   In the family, "three words need to be used.   I want to repeat this! Three words: 'Please', 'Thank you', 'Sorry'.   Three essential words!".[132]   "In our families when we are not overbearing and ask: 'May I?'; in our families when we are not selfish and can say: 'Thank you!'; and in our families when someone realizes that he or she did something wrong and is able to say 'Sorry!', our family

---

[132] *Address to the Pilgrimage of Families during the Year of Faith* (26 October 2013): AAS 105 (2013), 980.

experiences peace and joy".[133] Let us not be stingy about using these words, but keep repeating them, day after day. For "certain silences are oppressive, even at times within families, between husbands and wives, between parents and children, among siblings".[134] The right words, spoken at the right time, daily protect and nurture love.

134. All this occurs through a process of constant growth. The very special form of love that is marriage is called to embody what Saint Thomas Aquinas said about charity in general. "Charity", he says, "by its very nature, has no limit to its increase, for it is a participation in that infinite charity which is the Holy Spirit... Nor on the part of the subject can its limit be fixed, because as charity grows, so too does its capacity for an even greater increase".[135] Saint Paul also prays: "May the Lord make you increase and abound in love to one another" (*1 Th* 3:12), and again, "concerning fraternal love... we urge you, beloved, to do so more and more" (*1 Th* 4:9-10). More and more! Marital love is not defended primarily by presenting indissolubility as a duty, or by repeating doctrine, but by helping it to grow ever stronger under the impulse of grace. A love that fails to grow is at risk. Growth can only occur if we respond to God's grace through constant acts of love, acts of kindness that become ever more frequent,

[133] *Angelus Message* (29 December 2013): *L'Osservatore Romano*, 30-31 December 2013, p. 7.
[134] *Address to the Pilgrimage of Families during the Year of Faith* (26 October 2013): AAS 105 (2013), 978.
[135] *Summa Theologiae* II-II, q. 24, art. 7.

28

intense, generous, tender and cheerful. Husbands and wives "become conscious of their unity and experience it more deeply from day to day".[136] The gift of God's love poured out upon the spouses is also a summons to constant growth in grace.

135. It is not helpful to dream of an idyllic and perfect love needing no stimulus to grow. A celestial notion of earthly love forgets that the best is yet to come, that fine wine matures with age. As the Bishops of Chile have pointed out, "the perfect families proposed by deceptive consumerist propaganda do not exist. In those families, no one grows old, there is no sickness, sorrow or death... Consumerist propaganda presents a fantasy that has nothing to do with the reality which must daily be faced by the heads of families".[137] It is much healthier to be realistic about our limits, defects and imperfections, and to respond to the call to grow together, to bring love to maturity and to strengthen the union, come what may.

Dialogue

136. Dialogue is essential for experiencing, expressing and fostering love in marriage and family life. Yet it can only be the fruit of a long and demanding apprenticeship. Men and women, young people and adults, communicate differently. They speak different

---

[136] SECOND VATICAN ECUMENICAL COUNCIL, Pastoral Constitution on the Church in the Modern World *Gaudium et Spes*, 48.
[137] CHILEAN BISHOPS' CONFERENCE, *La vida y la familia: regalos de Dios para cada uno de nosotros* (21 July 2014).

languages and they act in different ways. Our way of asking and responding to questions, the tone we use, our timing and any number of other factors condition how well we communicate. We need to develop certain attitudes that express love and encourage authentic dialogue.

137. Take time, quality time. This means being ready to listen patiently and attentively to everything the other person wants to say. It requires the self-discipline of not speaking until the time is right. Instead of offering an opinion or advice, we need to be sure that we have heard everything the other person has to say. This means cultivating an interior silence that makes it possible to listen to the other person without mental or emotional distractions. Do not be rushed, put aside all of your own needs and worries, and make space. Often the other spouse does not need a solution to his or her problems, but simply to be heard, to feel that someone has acknowledged their pain, their disappointment, their fear, their anger, their hopes and their dreams. How often we hear complaints like: "He does not listen to me." "Even when you seem to, you are really doing something else." "I talk to her and I feel like she can't wait for me to finish." "When I speak to her, she tries to change the subject, or she gives me curt responses to end the conversation".

138. Develop the habit of giving real importance to the other person. This means appreciating them and recognizing their right to exist, to think as they do and

to be happy. Never downplay what they say or think, even if you need to express your own point of view. Everyone has something to contribute, because they have their life experiences, they look at things from a different standpoint and they have their own concerns, abilities and insights. We ought to be able to acknowledge the other person's truth, the value of his or her deepest concerns, and what it is that they are trying to communicate, however aggressively. We have to put ourselves in their shoes and try to peer into their hearts, to perceive their deepest concerns and to take them as a point of departure for further dialogue.

139. Keep an open mind. Don't get bogged down in your own limited ideas and opinions, but be prepared to change or expand them. The combination of two different ways of thinking can lead to a synthesis that enriches both. The unity that we seek is not uniformity, but a "unity in diversity", or "reconciled diversity". Fraternal communion is enriched by respect and appreciation for differences within an overall perspective that advances the common good. We need to free ourselves from feeling that we all have to be alike. A certain astuteness is also needed to prevent the appearance of "static" that can interfere with the process of dialogue. For example, if hard feelings start to emerge, they should be dealt with sensitively, lest they interrupt the dynamic of dialogue. The ability to say what one is thinking without offending the other person is important. Words should be carefully chosen so as not to offend, especially when discussing difficult issues. Making a

point should never involve venting anger and inflicting hurt. A patronizing tone only serves to hurt, ridicule, accuse and offend others. Many disagreements between couples are not about important things. Mostly they are about trivial matters. What alters the mood, however, is the way things are said or the attitude with which they are said.

140. Show affection and concern for the other person. Love surmounts even the worst barriers. When we love someone, or when we feel loved by them, we can better understand what they are trying to communicate. Fearing the other person as a kind of "rival" is a sign of weakness and needs to be overcome. It is very important to base one's position on solid choices, beliefs or values, and not on the need to win an argument or to be proved right.

141. Finally, let us acknowledge that for a worthwhile dialogue we have to have something to say. This can only be the fruit of an interior richness nourished by reading, personal reflection, prayer and openness to the world around us. Otherwise, conversations become boring and trivial. When neither of the spouses works at this, and has little real contact with other people, family life becomes stifling and dialogue impoverished.

Passionate love

142. The Second Vatican Council teaches that this conjugal love "embraces the good of the whole person; it can enrich the sentiments of the spirit and

their physical expression with a unique dignity and ennoble them as the special features and manifestation of the friendship proper to marriage".[138] For this reason, a love lacking either pleasure or passion is insufficient to symbolize the union of the human heart with God: "All the mystics have affirmed that supernatural love and heavenly love find the symbols which they seek in marital love, rather than in friendship, filial devotion or devotion to a cause. And the reason is to be found precisely in its totality".[139] Why then should we not pause to speak of feelings and sexuality in marriage?

The world of emotions

143. Desires, feelings, emotions, what the ancients called "the passions", all have an important place in married life. They are awakened whenever "another" becomes present and part of a person's life. It is characteristic of all living beings to reach out to other things, and this tendency always has basic affective signs: pleasure or pain, joy or sadness, tenderness or fear. They ground the most elementary psychological activity. Human beings live on this earth, and all that they do and seek is fraught with passion.

---

[138] Pastoral Constitution on the Church in the Modern World *Gaudium et Spes*, 49.

[139] A. SERTILLANGES, *L'Amour chrétien*, Paris, 1920, 174.

144. As true man, Jesus showed his emotions. He was hurt by the rejection of Jerusalem (cf. *Mt* 23:27) and this moved him to tears (cf. *Lk* 19:41). He was also deeply moved by the sufferings of others (cf. *Mk* 6:34). He felt deeply their grief (cf. *Jn* 11:33), and he wept at the death of a friend (cf. *Jn* 11:35). These examples of his sensitivity showed how much his human heart was open to others.

145. Experiencing an emotion is not, in itself, morally good or evil.[140] The stirring of desire or repugnance is neither sinful nor blameworthy. What is morally good or evil is what we do on the basis of, or under the influence of, a given passion. But when passions are aroused or sought, and as a result we perform evil acts, the evil lies in the decision to fuel them and in the evil acts that result. Along the same lines, my being attracted to someone is not automatically good. If my attraction to that person makes me try to dominate him or her, then my feeling only serves my selfishness. To believe that we are good simply because "we feel good" is a tremendous illusion. There are those who feel themselves capable of great love only because they have a great need for affection, yet they prove incapable of the effort needed to bring happiness to others. They remain caught up in their own needs and desires. In such cases, emotions distract from the highest values and conceal a self-centredness that makes it impossible to develop a healthy and happy family life.

---

[140] Cf. Thomas Aquinas, *Summa Theologiae* I-II, q. 24, art. 1.

146. This being said, if passion accompanies a free act, it can manifest the depth of that act. Marital love strives to ensure that one's entire emotional life benefits the family as a whole and stands at the service of its common life. A family is mature when the emotional life of its members becomes a form of sensitivity that neither stifles nor obscures great decisions and values, but rather follows each one's freedom,[141] springs from it, enriches, perfects and harmonizes it in the service of all.

God loves the joy of his children

147. This calls for a pedagogical process that involves renunciation. This conviction on the part of the Church has often been rejected as opposed to human happiness. Benedict XVI summed up this charge with great clarity: "Doesn't the Church, with all her commandments and prohibitions, turn to bitterness the most precious thing in life? Doesn't she blow the whistle just when the joy which is the Creator's gift offers us a happiness which is itself a certain foretaste of the Divine?"[142] He responded that, although there have been exaggerations and deviant forms of asceticism in Christianity, the Church's official teaching, in fidelity to the Scriptures, did not reject "*eros* as such, but rather declared war on a warped and destructive form of it, because this

---

[141] Cf. *ibid.*, q. 59, art. 5.
[142] Encyclical Letter *Deus Caritas Est* (25 December 2005), 3: AAS 98 (2006), 219-220.

counterfeit divinization of *eros*... actually strips it of divine dignity and dehumanizes it".[143]

148.   Training in the areas of emotion and instinct is necessary, and at times this requires setting limits. Excess, lack of control or obsession with a single form of pleasure can end up weakening and tainting that very pleasure[144] and damaging family life. A person can certainly channel his passions in a beautiful and healthy way, increasingly pointing them towards altruism and an integrated self-fulfilment that can only enrich interpersonal relationships in the heart of the family. This does not mean renouncing moments of intense enjoyment,[145] but rather integrating them with other moments of generous commitment, patient hope, inevitable weariness and struggle to achieve an ideal. Family life is all this, and it deserves to be lived to the fullest.

149.   Some currents of spirituality teach that desire has to be eliminated as a path to liberation from pain. Yet we believe that God loves the enjoyment felt by human beings: he created us and "richly furnishes us with everything to enjoy" (*1 Tim* 6:17). Let us be glad when with great love he tells us: "My son, treat yourself well... Do not deprive yourself of a happy day" (*Sir* 14:11-14). Married couples like-

---

[143] *Ibid.*, 4: AAS 98 (2006), 220.

[144] Cf. Thomas Aquinas, *Summa Theologiae* I-II, q. 32, art. 7.

[145] Cf. Id., *Summa Theologiae* II-II, q. 153, art. 2, ad 2: "*Abundantia delectationis quae est in actu venereo secundum rationem ordinato, non contrariatur medio virtutis*".

wise respond to God's will when they take up the biblical injunction: "Be joyful in the day of prosperity" (*Ec* 7:14). What is important is to have the freedom to realize that pleasure can find different expressions at different times of life, in accordance with the needs of mutual love. In this sense, we can appreciate the teachings of some Eastern masters who urge us to expand our consciousness, lest we be imprisoned by one limited experience that can blinker us. This expansion of consciousness is not the denial or destruction of desire so much as its broadening and perfection.

The erotic dimension of love

150.   All this brings us to the sexual dimension of marriage. God himself created sexuality, which is a marvellous gift to his creatures. If this gift needs to be cultivated and directed, it is to prevent the "impoverishment of an authentic value".[146]   Saint John Paul II rejected the claim that the Church's teaching is "a negation of the value of human sexuality", or that the Church simply tolerates sexuality "because it is necessary for procreation".[147]   Sexual desire is not something to be looked down upon, and "and there can be no attempt whatsoever to call into question its necessity".[148]

---

[146]   JOHN PAUL II, Catechesis (22 October 1980), 5: *Insegnamenti* III/2 (1980), 951.

[147]   *Ibid.*, 3.

[148]   ID., Catechesis, (24 September 1980), 4: *Insegnamenti* III/2 (1980), 719.

151. To those who fear that the training of the passions and of sexuality detracts from the spontaneity of sexual love, Saint John Paul II replied that human persons are "called to full and mature spontaneity in their relationships", a maturity that "is the gradual fruit of a discernment of the impulses of one's own heart".[149] This calls for discipline and self-mastery, since every human person "must learn, with perseverance and consistency, the meaning of his or her body".[150] Sexuality is not a means of gratification or entertainment; it is an interpersonal language wherein the other is taken seriously, in his or her sacred and inviolable dignity. As such, "the human heart comes to participate, so to speak, in another kind of spontaneity".[151] In this context, the erotic appears as a specifically human manifestation of sexuality. It enables us to discover "the nuptial meaning of the body and the authentic dignity of the gift".[152] In his catecheses on the theology of the body, Saint John Paul II taught that sexual differentiation not only is "a source of fruitfulness and procreation", but also possesses "the capacity of expressing love: that love precisely in which the human person becomes a gift".[153] A healthy sexual desire, albeit closely joined to a pursuit of pleasure, always involves

[149] Catechesis (12 November 1980), 2: *Insegnamenti* III/2 (1980), 1133.
[150] *Ibid.*, 4.
[151] *Ibid.*, 5.
[152] *Ibid.*, 1: 1132.
[153] Catechesis (16 January 1980), 1: *Insegnamenti* III/1 (1980), 151.

a sense of wonder, and for that very reason can humanize the impulses.

152.   In no way, then, can we consider the erotic dimension of love simply as a permissible evil or a burden to be tolerated for the good of the family. Rather, it must be seen as gift from God that enriches the relationship of the spouses. As a passion sublimated by a love respectful of the dignity of the other, it becomes a "pure, unadulterated affirmation" revealing the marvels of which the human heart is capable. In this way, even momentarily, we can feel that "life has turned out good and happy".[154]

Violence and manipulation

153.   On the basis of this positive vision of sexuality, we can approach the entire subject with a healthy realism.   It is, after all, a fact that sex often becomes depersonalized and unhealthy; as a result, "it becomes the occasion and instrument for self-assertion and the selfish satisfaction of personal desires and instincts".[155] In our own day, sexuality risks being poisoned by the mentality of "use and discard".   The body of the other is often viewed as an object to be used as long as it offers satisfaction, and rejected once it is no longer appealing.   Can we really ignore or overlook the continuing forms of domination, arrogance, abuse,

[154] Josef Pieper, *Über die Liebe*, Munich, 2014, 174. English: *On Love*, in *Faith, Hope, Love*, San Francisco, 1997, p. 256.
[155] John Paul II, Encyclical Letter *Evangelium Vitae* (25 March 1995), 23: AAS 87 (1995), 427.

sexual perversion and violence that are the product of a warped understanding of sexuality? Or the fact that the dignity of others and our human vocation to love thus end up being less important than an obscure need to "find oneself"?

154. We also know that, within marriage itself, sex can become a source of suffering and manipulation. Hence it must be clearly reaffirmed that "a conjugal act imposed on one's spouse without regard to his or her condition, or personal and reasonable wishes in the matter, is no true act of love, and therefore offends the moral order in its particular application to the intimate relationship of husband and wife".[156] The acts proper to the sexual union of husband and wife correspond to the nature of sexuality as willed by God when they take place in "a manner which is truly human".[157] Saint Paul insists: "Let no one transgress and wrong his brother or sister in this matter" (*1 Th* 4:6). Even though Paul was writing in the context of a patriarchal culture in which women were considered completely subordinate to men, he nonetheless taught that sex must involve communication between the spouses: he brings up the possibility of postponing sexual relations for a period, but "by agreement" (*1 Cor* 7:5).

[156] PAUL VI, Encyclical Letter *Humanae Vitae* (25 July 1968), 13: AAS 60 (1968), 489.
[157] SECOND VATICAN ECUMENICAL COUNCIL, Pastoral Constitution on the Church in the Modern World *Gaudium et Spes*, 49.

155. Saint John Paul II very subtly warned that a couple can be "threatened by insatiability"[158]. In other words, while called to an increasingly profound union, they can risk effacing their differences and the rightful distance between the two. For each possesses his or her own proper and inalienable dignity. When reciprocal belonging turns into domination, "the structure of communion in interpersonal relations is essentially changed".[159] It is part of the mentality of domination that those who dominate end up negating their own dignity.[160] Ultimately, they no longer "identify themselves subjectively with their own body",[161] because they take away its deepest meaning. They end up using sex as a form of escapism and renounce the beauty of conjugal union.

156. Every form of sexual submission must be clearly rejected. This includes all improper interpretations of the passage in the Letter to the Ephesians where Paul tells women to "be subject to your husbands" (*Eph* 5:22). This passage mirrors the cultural categories of the time, but our concern is not with its cultural matrix but with the revealed message that it conveys. As Saint John Paul II wisely observed: "Love excludes every kind of subjection whereby the wife might become a servant or a slave of the husband... The community or unity which they should establish

---

[158] Catechesis (18 June 1980), 5: *Insegnamenti* III/1 (1980), 1778.
[159] *Ibid.*, 6.
[160] Cf. Catechesis (30 July 1980), 1: *Insegnamenti* III/2 (1980), 311.
[161] Catechesis (8 April 1981), 3: *Insegnamenti* IV/1 (1981), 904.

through marriage is constituted by a reciprocal donation of self, which is also a mutual subjection".[162]
Hence Paul goes on to say that "husbands should love
their wives as their own bodies" (*Eph* 5:28). The biblical text is actually concerned with encouraging
everyone to overcome a complacent individualism
and to be constantly mindful of others: "Be subject
to one another" (*Eph* 5:21). In marriage, this
reciprocal "submission" takes on a special meaning,
and is seen as a freely chosen mutual belonging
marked by fidelity, respect and care. Sexuality is
inseparably at the service of this conjugal friendship, for it is meant to aid the fulfilment of the
other.

157. All the same, the rejection of distortions of
sexuality and eroticism should never lead us to a dis-
paragement or neglect of sexuality and *eros* in themselves. The ideal of marriage cannot be seen purely as
generous donation and self-sacrifice, where each
spouse renounces all personal needs and seeks only
the other's good without concern for personal satisfaction. We need to remember that authentic love
also needs to be able to receive the other, to accept
one's own vulnerability and needs, and to welcome
with sincere and joyful gratitude the physical expressions of love found in a caress, an embrace, a kiss and
sexual union. Benedict XVI stated this very clearly:
"Should man aspire to be pure spirit and to reject the

---

[162] Catechesis (11 August 1982), 4: *Insegnamenti* V/3 (1982), 205-206.

flesh as pertaining to his animal nature alone, then spirit and body would both lose their dignity".[163] For this reason, "man cannot live by oblative, descending love alone. He cannot always give, he must also receive. Anyone who wishes to give love must also receive love as a gift".[164] Still, we must never forget that our human equilibrium is fragile; there is a part of us that resists real human growth, and any moment it can unleash the most primitive and selfish tendencies.

THE TRANSFORMATION OF LOVE

163.   Longer life spans now mean that close and exclusive relationships must last for four, five or even six decades; consequently, the initial decision has to be frequently renewed. While one of the spouses may no longer experience an intense sexual desire for the other, he or she may still experience the pleasure of mutual belonging and the knowledge that neither of them is alone but has a "partner" with whom everything in life is shared. He or she is a companion on life's journey, one with whom to face life's difficulties and enjoy its pleasures. This satisfaction is part of the affection proper to conjugal love. There is no guarantee that we will feel the same way all through life. Yet if a couple can come up with a shared and lasting life project, they can love one another and live as one until death do them part, enjoying an enriching intimacy.

[163] Encyclical Letter *Deus Caritas Est* (25 December 2005), 5: AAS 98 (2006), 221.
[164] *Ibid.*, 7.

The love they pledge is greater than any emotion, feeling or state of mind, although it may include all of these. It is a deeper love, a lifelong decision of the heart. Even amid unresolved conflicts and confused emotional situations, they daily reaffirm their decision to love, to belong to one another, to share their lives and to continue loving and forgiving. Each progresses along the path of personal growth and development. On this journey, love rejoices at every step and in every new stage.

164.   In the course of every marriage physical appearances change, but this hardly means that love and attraction need fade. We love the other person for who they are, not simply for their body. Although the body ages, it still expresses that personal identity that first won our heart. Even if others can no longer see the beauty of that identity, a spouse continues to see it with the eyes of love and so his or her affection does not diminish. He or she reaffirms the decision to belong to the other and expresses that choice in faithful and loving closeness. The nobility of this decision, by its intensity and depth, gives rise to a new kind of emotion as they fulfil their marital mission. For "emotion, caused by another human being as a person... does not *per se* tend toward the conjugal act".[174] It finds other sensible expressions. Indeed, love "is a single reality, but with different dimensions; at different times, one or other

---

[174]   JOHN PAUL II, Catechesis (31 October 1984), 6: *Insegnamenti* VII/2 (1984), 1072.

dimension may emerge more clearly".[175] The marriage bond finds new forms of expression and constantly seeks new ways to grow in strength. These both preserve and strengthen the bond. They call for daily effort. None of this, however, is possible without praying to the Holy Spirit for an outpouring of his grace, his supernatural strength and his spiritual fire, to confirm, direct and transform our love in every new situation.

---

[175] BENEDICT XVI, Encyclical Letter *Deus Caritas Est* (25 December 2005), 8: AAS 98 (2006), 224.

LOVE MADE FRUITFUL

165.   Love always gives life. Conjugal love "does not end with the couple... The couple, in giving themselves to one another, give not just themselves but also the reality of children, who are a living reflection of their love, a permanent sign of their conjugal unity and a living and inseparable synthesis of their being a father and a mother".[176]

Welcoming a new life

166.   The family is the setting in which a new life is not only born but also welcomed as a gift of God. Each new life "allows us to appreciate the utterly gratuitous dimension of love, which never ceases to amaze us. It is the beauty of being loved first: children are loved even before they arrive".[177] Here we see a reflection of the primacy of the love of God, who always takes the initiative, for children "are loved before having done

---

[176] JOHN PAUL II, Apostolic Exhortation *Familiaris Consortio*, (22 November 1981), 14: AAS 74 (1982), 96.
[177] Catechesis (11 February 2015): *L'Osservatore Romano*, 12 February 2015, p. 8.

anything to deserve it".[178] And yet, "from the first moments of their lives, many children are rejected, abandoned, and robbed of their childhood and future. There are those who dare to say, as if to justify themselves, that it was a mistake to bring these children into the world. This is shameful! ... How can we issue solemn declarations on human rights and the rights of children, if we then punish children for the errors of adults?"[179] If a child comes into this world in unwanted circumstances, the parents and other members of the family must do everything possible to accept that child as a gift from God and assume the responsibility of accepting him or her with openness and affection. For "when speaking of children who come into the world, no sacrifice made by adults will be considered too costly or too great, if it means the child never has to feel that he or she is a mistake, or worthless or abandoned to the four winds and the arrogance of man".[180] The gift of a new child, entrusted by the Lord to a father and a mother, begins with acceptance, continues with lifelong protection and has as its final goal the joy of eternal life. By serenely contemplating the ultimate fulfilment of each human person, parents will be even more aware of the precious gift entrusted to them. For God allows

[178] *Ibid.*
[179] Catechesis (8 April 2015): *L'Osservatore Romano*, 9 April 2015, p. 8.
[180] *Ibid.*

parents to choose the name by which he himself will call their child for all eternity.[181]

167.   Large families are a joy for the Church. They are an expression of the fruitfulness of love. At the same time, Saint John Paul II rightly explained that responsible parenthood does not mean "unlimited procreation or lack of awareness of what is involved in rearing children, but rather the empowerment of couples to use their inviolable liberty wisely and responsibly, taking into account social and demographic realities, as well as their own situation and legitimate desires".[182]

Love and pregnancy

168.   Pregnancy is a difficult but wonderful time. A mother joins with God to bring forth the miracle of a new life. Motherhood is the fruit of a "particular creative potential of the female body, directed to the conception and birth of a new human being".[183]   Each woman shares in "the mystery of creation, which is

[181] Cf. Second Vatican Ecumenical Council, Pastoral Constitution on the Church in the Modern World *Gaudium et Spes*, 51: "Let us all be convinced that human life and its transmission are realities whose meaning is not limited by the horizons of this life only: their true evaluation and full meaning can only be understood in reference to our eternal destiny".

[182] *Letter to the Secretary General of the United Nations Organization on Population and Development* (18 March 1994): *Insegnamenti* XVII/1 (1994), 750-751.

[183] John Paul II, Catechesis (12 March 1980), 3: *Insegnamenti* III/1 (1980), 543.

renewed with each birth".[184] The Psalmist says: "You knit me together in my mother's womb" (*Ps* 139:13). Every child growing within the mother's womb is part of the eternal loving plan of God the Father: "Before I formed you in the womb I knew you, and before you were born I consecrated you" (*Jer* 1:5). Each child has a place in God's heart from all eternity; once he or she is conceived, the Creator's eternal dream comes true. Let us pause to think of the great value of that embryo from the moment of conception. We need to see it with the eyes of God, who always looks beyond mere appearances.

169.   A pregnant woman can participate in God's plan by dreaming of her child. "For nine months every mother and father dreams about their child… You can't have a family without dreams. Once a family loses the ability to dream, children do not grow, love does not grow, life shrivels up and dies".[185] For Christian married couples, baptism necessarily appears as a part of that dream. With their prayers, parents prepare for baptism, entrusting their baby to Jesus even before he or she is born.

170.   Scientific advances today allow us to know beforehand what colour a child's hair will be or what illnesses they may one day suffer, because all the somatic traits of the person are written in his or her

[184] *Ibid.*
[185] *Address at the Meeting with Families in Manila* (16 January 2015): AAS 107 (2015), 176.

genetic code already in the embryonic stage. Yet only the Father, the Creator, fully knows the child; he alone knows his or her deepest identity and worth. Expectant mothers need to ask God for the wisdom fully to know their children and to accept them as they are. Some parents feel that their child is not coming at the best time. They should ask the Lord to heal and strengthen them to accept their child fully and wholeheartedly. It is important for that child to feel wanted. He or she is not an accessory or a solution to some personal need. A child is a human being of immense worth and may never be used for one's own benefit. So it matters little whether this new life is convenient for you, whether it has features that please you, or whether it fits into your plans and aspirations. For "children are a gift. Each one is unique and irreplaceable... We love our children because they are children, not because they are beautiful, or look or think as we do, or embody our dreams. We love them because they are children. A child is a child".[186] The love of parents is the means by which God our Father shows his own love. He awaits the birth of each child, accepts that child unconditionally, and welcomes him or her freely.

171.   With great affection I urge all future mothers: keep happy and let nothing rob you of the interior joy of motherhood. Your child deserves your happiness. Don't let fears, worries, other people's comments or

[186] Catechesis (11 February 2015): *L'Osservatore Romano*, 12 February 2015, p. 8.

problems lessen your joy at being God's means of bringing a new life to the world. Prepare yourself for the birth of your child, but without obsessing, and join in Mary's song of joy: "My soul proclaims the greatness of the Lord and my spirit exults in God my Saviour, for he has looked with favour on the lowliness of his servant" (*Lk* 1:46-48). Try to experience this serene excitement amid all your many concerns, and ask the Lord to preserve your joy, so that you can pass it on to your child.

The love of a mother and a father

172. "Children, once born, begin to receive, along with nourishment and care, the spiritual gift of knowing with certainty that they are loved. This love is shown to them through the gift of their personal name, the sharing of language, looks of love and the brightness of a smile. In this way, they learn that the beauty of human relationships touches our soul, seeks our freedom, accepts the difference of others, recognizes and respects them as a partner in dialogue... Such is love, and it contains a spark of God's love!"[187] Every child has a right to receive love from a mother and a father; both are necessary for a child's integral and harmonious development. As the Australian Bishops have observed, each of the spouses "contributes in a distinct way to the upbringing of a child. Respecting a child's dignity means affirming his or her need and natural

---

[187] Catechesis (14 October 2015): *L'Osservatore Romano*, 15 October 2015, p. 8.

right to have a mother and a father".[188] We are speaking not simply of the love of father and mother as individuals, but also of their mutual love, perceived as the source of one's life and the solid foundation of the family. Without this, a child could become a mere plaything. Husband and wife, father and mother, both "cooperate with the love of God the Creator, and are, in a certain sense, his interpreters".[189] They show their children the maternal and paternal face of the Lord. Together they teach the value of reciprocity, of respect for differences and of being able to give and take. If for some inevitable reason one parent should be lacking, it is important to compensate for this loss, for the sake of the child's healthy growth to maturity.

173.   The sense of being orphaned that affects many children and young people today is much deeper than we think. Nowadays we acknowledge as legitimate and indeed desirable that women wish to study, work, develop their skills and have personal goals. At the same time, we cannot ignore the need that children have for a mother's presence, especially in the first months of life. Indeed, "the woman stands before the man as a mother, the subject of the new human life that is conceived and develops in her, and from her is born into the world".[190] The weakening of this

[188] AUSTRALIAN CATHOLIC BISHOPS' CONFERENCE, Pastoral Letter *Don't Mess with Marriage* (24 November 2015), 13.
[189] SECOND VATICAN ECUMENICAL COUNCIL, Pastoral Constitution on the Church in the Modern World *Gaudium et Spes*, 50.
[190] JOHN PAUL II, Catechesis (12 March 1980), 2: *Insegnamenti* III/1 (1980), 542.

maternal presence with its feminine qualities poses a grave risk to our world. I certainly value feminism, but one that does not demand uniformity or negate motherhood. For the grandeur of women includes all the rights derived from their inalienable human dignity but also from their feminine genius, which is essential to society. Their specifically feminine abilities – motherhood in particular – also grant duties, because womanhood also entails a specific mission in this world, a mission that society needs to protect and preserve for the good of all.[191]

174. "Mothers are the strongest antidote to the spread of self-centred individualism... It is they who testify to the beauty of life".[192] Certainly, "a society without mothers would be dehumanized, for mothers are always, even in the worst of times, witnesses to tenderness, dedication and moral strength. Mothers often communicate the deepest meaning of religious practice in the first prayers and acts of devotion that their children learn... Without mothers, not only would there be no new faithful, but the faith itself would lose a good part of its simple and profound warmth... Dear mothers: thank you! Thank you for what you are in your family and for what you give to the Church and the world".[193]

---

[191] Cf. Id., Apostolic Letter *Mulieris Dignitatem* (15 August 1988), 30-31: AAS 80 (1988), 1726-1729.
[192] Catechesis (7 January 2015): *L'Osservatore Romano*, 7-8 January 2015, p. 8.
[193] *Ibid.*

175. A mother who watches over her child with tenderness and compassion helps him or her to grow in confidence and to experience that the world is a good and welcoming place. This helps the child to grow in self-esteem and, in turn, to develop a capacity for intimacy and empathy. A father, for his part, helps the child to perceive the limits of life, to be open to the challenges of the wider world, and to see the need for hard work and strenuous effort. A father possessed of a clear and serene masculine identity who demonstrates affection and concern for his wife is just as necessary as a caring mother. There can be a certain flexibility of roles and responsibilities, depending on the concrete circumstances of each particular family. But the clear and well-defined presence of both figures, female and male, creates the environment best suited to the growth of the child.

176. We often hear that ours is "a society without fathers". In Western culture, the father figure is said to be symbolically absent, missing or vanished. Manhood itself seems to be called into question. The result has been an understandable confusion. "At first, this was perceived as a liberation: liberation from the father as master, from the father as the representative of a law imposed from without, from the father as the arbiter of his children's happiness and an obstacle to the emancipation and autonomy of young people. In some homes authoritarianism once reigned and, at

times, even oppression".[194] Yet, "as often happens, one goes from one extreme to the other. In our day, the problem no longer seems to be the overbearing presence of the father so much as his absence, his not being there. Fathers are often so caught up in themselves and their work, and at times in their own self-fulfilment, that they neglect their families. They leave the little ones and the young to themselves".[195] The presence of the father, and hence his authority, is also impacted by the amount of time given over to the communications and entertainment media. Nowadays authority is often considered suspect and adults treated with impertinence. They themselves become uncertain and so fail to offer sure and solid guidance to their children. A reversal of the roles of parents and children is unhealthy, since it hinders the proper process of development that children need to experience, and it denies them the love and guidance needed to mature.[196]

177. God sets the father in the family so that by the gifts of his masculinity he can be "close to his wife and share everything, joy and sorrow, hope and hardship. And to be close to his children as they grow – when they play and when they work, when they are carefree and when they are distressed, when they are talkative and when they are silent, when they

---

[194] Catechesis (28 January 2015): *L'Osservatore Romano*, 29 January 2015, p. 8.
[195] *Ibid.*
[196] Cf. *Relatio Finalis* 2015, 28.

are daring and when they are afraid, when they stray and when they get back on the right path. To be a father who is always present. When I say 'present', I do not mean 'controlling'. Fathers who are too controlling overshadow their children, they don't let them develop".[197] Some fathers feel they are useless or unnecessary, but the fact is that "children need to find a father waiting for them when they return home with their problems. They may try hard not to admit it, not to show it, but they need it".[198] It is not good for children to lack a father and to grow up before they are ready.

AN EXPANDING FRUITFULNESS

178.   Some couples are unable to have children. We know that this can be a cause of real suffering for them. At the same time, we know that "marriage was not instituted solely for the procreation of children… Even in cases where, despite the intense desire of the spouses, there are no children, marriage still retains its character of being a whole manner and communion of life, and preserves its value and indissolubility".[199] So too, "motherhood is not a solely biological reality, but is expressed in diverse ways".[200]

---

[197] Catechesis (4 February 2015), *L'Osservatore Romano*, 5 February 2015, p. 8.
[198] *Ibid.*
[199] SECOND VATICAN ECUMENICAL COUNCIL, Pastoral Constitution on the Church in the Modern World *Gaudium et Spes*, 50.
[200] FIFTH GENERAL CONFERENCE OF THE LATIN AMERICAN AND CARIBBEAN BISHOPS, *Aparecida Document* (29 June 2007), No. 457.

179.   Adoption is a very generous way to become parents. I encourage those who cannot have children to expand their marital love to embrace those who lack a proper family situation. They will never regret having been generous. Adopting a child is an act of love, offering the gift of a family to someone who has none. It is important to insist that legislation help facilitate the adoption process, above all in the case of unwanted children, in order to prevent their abortion or abandonment. Those who accept the challenge of adopting and accepting someone unconditionally and gratuitously become channels of God's love. For he says, "Even if your mother forgets you, I will not forget you" (*Is* 49:15).

180.   "The choice of adoption and foster care expresses a particular kind of fruitfulness in the marriage experience, and not only in cases of infertility. In the light of those situations where a child is desired at any cost, as a right for one's self-fulfilment, adoption and foster care, correctly understood, manifest an important aspect of parenting and the raising of children. They make people aware that children, whether natural, adoptive or taken in foster care, are persons in their own right who need to be accepted, loved and cared for, and not just brought into this world. The best interests of the child should always underlie any decision in adoption and foster care".[201] On the other hand, "the trafficking of children between

---

[201]   *Relatio Finalis* 2015, 65.

countries and continents needs to be prevented by appropriate legislative action and state control".[202]

181. We also do well to remember that procreation and adoption are not the only ways of experiencing the fruitfulness of love. Even large families are called to make their mark on society, finding other expressions of fruitfulness that in some way prolong the love that sustains them. Christian families should never forget that "faith does not remove us from the world, but draws us more deeply into it... Each of us, in fact, has a special role in preparing for the coming of God's kingdom in our world".[203] Families should not see themselves as a refuge from society, but instead go forth from their homes in a spirit of solidarity with others. In this way, they become a hub for integrating persons into society and a point of contact between the public and private spheres. Married couples should have a clear awareness of their social obligations. With this, their affection does not diminish but is flooded with new light. As the poet says:

"Your hands are my caress,
The harmony that fills my days.
I love you because your hands
Work for justice.

If I love you, it is because you are
My love, my companion and my all,

[202] *Ibid.*
[203] *Address at the Meeting with Families in Manila* (16 January 2015): AAS 107 (2015), 178.

And on the street, side by side,
We are much more than just two".[204]

182.   No family can be fruitful if it sees itself as
overly different or "set apart". To avoid this risk, we
should remember that Jesus' own family, so full of
grace and wisdom, did not appear unusual or different from others. That is why people found it hard to
acknowledge Jesus' wisdom: "Where did this man get
all this? Is not this the carpenter, the son of Mary?"
(*Mk* 6:2-3).   "Is this not the carpenter's son?"
(*Mt* 13:55). These questions make it clear that theirs
was an ordinary family, close to others, a normal part
of the community. Jesus did not grow up in a narrow
and stifling relationship with Mary and Joseph, but
readily interacted with the wider family, the relatives
of his parents and their friends. This explains how, on
returning from Jerusalem, Mary and Joseph could
imagine for a whole day that the twelve-year-old Jesus
was somewhere in the caravan, listening to people's
stories and sharing their concerns: "Supposing him to
be in the group of travellers, they went a day's journey"
(*Lk* 2:44).   Still, some Christian families, whether
because of the language they use, the way they act or
treat others, or their constant harping on the same
two or three issues, end up being seen as remote and

[204] Mario Benedetti, "Te Quiero", in *Poemas de otros*, Buenos
Aires 1993, 316: *"Tus manos son mi caricia / mis acordes cotidianos /
te quiero porque tus manos / trabajan por la justicia. // Si te quiero es
porque sos / mi amor mi cómplice y todo / y en la calle codo a codo / somos
mucho más que dos."*

not really a part of the community. Even their relatives feel looked down upon or judged by them.

183. A married couple who experience the power of love know that this love is called to bind the wounds of the outcast, to foster a culture of encounter and to fight for justice. God has given the family the job of "domesticating" the world[205] and helping each person to see fellow human beings as brothers and sisters. "An attentive look at the everyday life of today's men and women immediately shows the omnipresent need for a healthy injection of family spirit... Not only is the organization of ordinary life increasingly thwarted by a bureaucracy completely removed from fundamental human bonds, but even social and political mores show signs of degradation".[206] For their part, open and caring families find a place for the poor and build friendships with those less fortunate than themselves. In their efforts to live according to the Gospel, they are mindful of Jesus' words: "As you did it to one of the least of these my brethren, you did it to me (*Mt* 25:40)". In a very real way, their lives express what is asked of us all: "When you give a dinner or a banquet, do not invite your friends or your brothers or your kinsmen or rich neighbours, lest they also invite you in return, and you be repaid. But when you give a feast, invite

---

[205] Cf. Catechesis (16 September 2015): *L'Osservatore Romano*, 17 September 2015, p. 8.
[206] Catechesis (7 October 2015): *L'Osservatore Romano*, 9 October 2015, p. 8.

the poor, the maimed, the lame, the blind, and you will be blessed" (*Lk* 14:12-14). You will be blessed! Here is the secret to a happy family.

184.　By their witness as well as their words, families speak to others of Jesus. They pass on the faith, they arouse a desire for God and they reflect the beauty of the Gospel and its way of life. Christian marriages thus enliven society by their witness of fraternity, their social concern, their outspokenness on behalf of the underprivileged, their luminous faith and their active hope. Their fruitfulness expands and in countless ways makes God's love present in society.

Discerning the body

185.　Along these same lines, we do well to take seriously a biblical text usually interpreted outside of its context or in a generic sense, with the risk of overlooking its immediate and direct meaning, which is markedly social. I am speaking of *1 Cor* 11:17-34, where Saint Paul faces a shameful situation in the community. The wealthier members tended to discriminate against the poorer ones, and this carried over even to the *agape* meal that accompanied the celebration of the Eucharist. While the rich enjoyed their food, the poor looked on and went hungry: "One is hungry and another is drunk. Do you not have houses to eat and drink in? Or do you despise the Church of God and humiliate those who have nothing?" (vv. 21-22).

186. The Eucharist demands that we be members of the one body of the Church. Those who approach the Body and Blood of Christ may not wound that same Body by creating scandalous distinctions and divisions among its members. This is what it means to "discern" the body of the Lord, to acknowledge it with faith and charity both in the sacramental signs and in the community; those who fail to do so eat and drink judgement against themselves (cf. v. 29). The celebration of the Eucharist thus becomes a constant summons for everyone "to examine himself or herself" (v. 28), to open the doors of the family to greater fellowship with the underprivileged, and in this way to receive the sacrament of that eucharistic love which makes us one body. We must not forget that "the 'mysticism' of the sacrament has a social character".[207] When those who receive it turn a blind eye to the poor and suffering, or consent to various forms of division, contempt and inequality, the Eucharist is received unworthily. On the other hand, families who are properly disposed and receive the Eucharist regularly, reinforce their desire for fraternity, their social consciousness and their commitment to those in need.

LIFE IN THE WIDER FAMILY

187. The nuclear family needs to interact with the wider family made up of parents, aunts and uncles, cousins and even neighbours. This greater family

---

[207] BENEDICT XVI, Encyclical Letter *Deus Caritas Est* (25 December 2005), 14: AAS 98 (2006), 228.

may have members who require assistance, or at least companionship and affection, or consolation amid suffering.[208] The individualism so prevalent today can lead to creating small nests of security, where others are perceived as bothersome or a threat. Such isolation, however, cannot offer greater peace or happiness; rather, it straitens the heart of a family and makes its life all the more narrow.

Being sons and daughters

188. First, let us think of our parents. Jesus told the Pharisees that abandoning one's parents is contrary to God's law (cf. *Mk* 7:8-13). We do well to remember that each of us is a son or daughter. "Even if one becomes an adult, or an elderly person, even if one becomes a parent, if one occupies a position of responsibility, underneath all of this is still the identity of a child. We are all sons and daughters. And this always brings us back to the fact that we did not give ourselves life but that we received it. The great gift of life is the first gift that we received".[209]

189. Hence, "the fourth commandment asks children… to honour their father and mother (cf. *Ex* 20:12). This commandment comes immediately after those dealing with God himself. Indeed, it has to do with something sacred, something divine, something

---

[208] Cf. *Relatio Finalis* 2015, 11.
[209] Catechesis (18 March 2015): *L'Osservatore Romano*, 19 March 2015, p. 8.

at the basis of every other kind of human respect. The biblical formulation of the fourth commandment goes on to say: 'that your days may be long in the land which the Lord your God gives you'. The virtuous bond between generations is the guarantee of the future, and is the guarantee of a truly humane society. A society with children who do not honour parents is a society without honour... It is a society destined to be filled with surly and greedy young people".[210]

190.   There is, however, another side to the coin. As the word of God tells us, "a man leaves his father and his mother" (*Gen* 2:24). This does not always happen, and a marriage is hampered by the failure to make this necessary sacrifice and surrender. Parents must not be abandoned or ignored, but marriage itself demands that they be "left", so that the new home will be a true hearth, a place of security, hope and future plans, and the couple can truly become "one flesh" (*ibid.*). In some marriages, one spouse keeps secrets from the other, confiding them instead to his or her parents. As a result, the opinions of their parents become more important than the feelings and opinions of their spouse. This situation cannot go on for long, and even if it takes time, both spouses need to make the effort to grow in trust and communication. Marriage challenges husbands and wives to find new ways of being sons and daughters.

---

[210] Catechesis (11 February 2015): *L'Osservatore Romano*, 12 February 2015, p. 8.

The elderly

191.   "Do not cast me off in the time of old age; forsake me not when my strength is spent" (*Ps* 71:9). This is the plea of the elderly, who fear being forgotten and rejected. Just as God asks us to be his means of hearing the cry of the poor, so too he wants us to hear the cry of the elderly.[211] This represents a challenge to families and communities, since "the Church cannot and does not want to conform to a mentality of impatience, and much less of indifference and contempt, towards old age. We must reawaken the collective sense of gratitude, of appreciation, of hospitality, which makes the elderly feel like a living part of the community. Our elderly are men and women, fathers and mothers, who came before us on our own road, in our own house, in our daily battle for a worthy life".[212]   Indeed, "how I would like a Church that challenges the throw-away culture by the overflowing joy of a new embrace between young and old!"[213]

192.   Saint John Paul II asked us to be attentive to the role of the elderly in our families, because there are cultures which, "especially in the wake of disordered industrial and urban development, have both in the past and in the present set the elderly aside in

[211] Cf. *Relatio Finalis* 2015, 17-18.
[212] Catechesis (4 March 2015): *L'Osservatore Romano*, 5 March 2015, p. 8.
[213] Catechesis (11 March 2015): *L'Osservatore Romano*, 12 March 2015, p. 8.

unacceptable ways".[214] The elderly help us to appreciate "the continuity of the generations", by their "charism of bridging the gap".[215] Very often it is grandparents who ensure that the most important values are passed down to their grandchildren, and "many people can testify that they owe their initiation into the Christian life to their grandparents".[216] Their words, their affection or simply their presence help children to realize that history did not begin with them, that they are now part of an age-old pilgrimage and that they need to respect all that came before them. Those who would break all ties with the past will surely find it difficult to build stable relationships and to realize that reality is bigger than they are. "Attention to the elderly makes the difference in a society. Does a society show concern for the elderly? Does it make room for the elderly? Such a society will move forward if it respects the wisdom of the elderly".[217]

193. The lack of historical memory is a serious shortcoming in our society. A mentality that can only say, "Then was then, now is now", is ultimately immature. Knowing and judging past events is the only way to build a meaningful future. Memory is necessary for

[214] Apostolic Exhortation *Familiaris Consortio*, 27 (22 November 1981): AAS 74 (1982), 113.

[215] ID., *Address to Participants in the "International Forum on Active Aging"* (5 September 1980), 5: *Insegnamenti* III/2 (1980), 539.

[216] *Relatio Finalis* 2015, 18.

[217] Catechesis (4 March 2015): *L'Osservatore Romano*, 5 March 2015, p. 8.

growth: "Recall the former days" (*Heb* 10:32). Listening to the elderly tell their stories is good for children and young people; it makes them feel connected to the living history of their families, their neighborhoods and their country. A family that fails to respect and cherish its grandparents, who are its living memory, is already in decline, whereas a family that remembers has a future. "A society that has no room for the elderly or discards them because they create problems, has a deadly virus";[218] "it is torn from its roots".[219] Our contemporary experience of being orphans as a result of cultural discontinuity, uprootedness and the collapse of the certainties that shape our lives, challenges us to make our families places where children can sink roots in the rich soil of a collective history.

Being brothers and sisters

194. Relationships between brothers and sisters deepen with the passing of time, and "the bond of fraternity that forms in the family between children, if consolidated by an educational atmosphere of openness to others, is a great school of freedom and peace. In the family, we learn how to live as one. Perhaps we do not always think about this, but the family itself introduces fraternity into the world. From this initial experience of fraternity, nourished by affection and

---

[218] *Ibid.*
[219] *Address at the Meeting with the Elderly* (28 September 2014): *L'Osservatore Romano*, 29-30 September 2014, p. 7.

education at home, the style of fraternity radiates like a promise upon the whole of society".[220]

195. Growing up with brothers and sisters makes for a beautiful experience of caring for and helping one another. For "fraternity in families is especially radiant when we see the care, the patience, the affection that surround the little brother or sister who is frail, sick or disabled".[221] It must be acknowledged that "having a brother or a sister who loves you is a profound, precious and unique experience".[222] Children do need to be patiently taught to treat one another as brothers and sisters. This training, at times quite demanding, is a true school of socialization. In some countries, where it has become quite common to have only one child, the experience of being a brother or sister is less and less common. When it has been possible to have only one child, ways have to be found to ensure that he or she does not grow up alone or isolated.

A big heart

196. In addition to the small circle of the couple and their children, there is the larger family, which cannot be overlooked. Indeed, "the love between husband and wife and, in a derivative and broader way, the love between members of the same family – between parents and children, brothers and sisters

---

[220] Catechesis (18 February 2015): *L'Osservatore Romano*, 19 February 2015, p. 8.
[221] *Ibid.*
[222] *Ibid.*

and relatives and members of the household – is given life and sustenance by an unceasing inner dynamism leading the family to ever deeper and more intense communion, which is the foundation and soul of the community of marriage and the family".[223] Friends and other families are part of this larger family, as well as communities of families who support one another in their difficulties, their social commitments and their faith.

197. This larger family should provide love and support to teenage mothers, children without parents, single mothers left to raise children, persons with disabilities needing particular affection and closeness, young people struggling with addiction, the unmarried, separated or widowed who are alone, and the elderly and infirm who lack the support of their children. It should also embrace "even those who have made shipwreck of their lives".[224] This wider family can help make up for the shortcomings of parents, detect and report possible situations in which children suffer violence and even abuse, and provide wholesome love and family stability in cases when parents prove incapable of this.

198. Finally, we cannot forget that this larger family includes fathers-in-law, mothers-in-law and

---

[223] JOHN PAUL II, Apostolic Exhortation *Familiaris Consortio* (22 November 1981), 18: AAS 74 (1982), 101.
[224] Catechesis (7 October 2015): *L'Osservatore Romano*, 8 October 2015), p. 8.

all the relatives of the couple. One particularly delicate aspect of love is learning not to view these relatives as somehow competitors, threats or intruders. The conjugal union demands respect for their traditions and customs, an effort to understand their language and to refrain from criticism, caring for them and cherishing them while maintaining the legitimate privacy and independence of the couple. Being willing to do so is also an exquisite expression of generous love for one's spouse.